A CANDLE BENEATH MY BED

BETRAYAL

A CANDLE BENEATH MY BED

BETRAYAL

Sandra D. Scott Johnson

ARPress
ILLUMINATING IDEAS.
EMPOWERING VOICES.

ARPress
45 Dan Road Suite 5
Canton MA 02021

Hotline: 1(888) 821-0229
Fax: 1(508) 545-7580

Ordering Information:
Quantity sales. Special discounts are available on quantity purchases by corporations, associations, and others. For details, contact the publisher at the address above.

Printed in the United States of America.

ISBN-13:	Paperback	979-8-89389-222-2
	eBook	979-8-89389-223-9
	Hardback	979-8-89389-224-6

Library of Congress Control Number: 2024904566

Table of Contents

Chapter 1

Tears within Tears

Waking up to the sounds of roosters crowing and trains roaring over the tracks was something that was a part of our lives. The sunlight seemed so bright, blazing through the holes and cracks in the walls and floors of a tiny four-room house that sat on the hillside. It seemed like the house was barely standing, but it was home to us.

Not only did you see cracks and holes, but you could see the ground through the floors as well. The seasons in Savannah Georgia were sometimes picture-perfect, but the days were very hot, and the nights were long, hot, and miserable during the summer months. There was no air conditioning, because there was no electricity in our home. Sometimes leaving a small crack in the window at night a small amount of cool air may flow through just a little.

During the winter months, the days and nights were very cold. The only prefect part was the nights, when the stars shone bright and the air was fresh and clean. Lying in bed, to the sounds of whooping birds and crickets was beautiful music to my ears.

Here in Savannah, in a small neighborhood, lived the Jones family; we were very close and loved one another. Everyone basically knew what was happening to each other; although, in this case, no one had any idea about the deep dark secrets that were hidden behind the walls of my home.

On a very cold winter night, I, Jacqueline (Jackie for short), was born to the proud parents of Ruth Green and Matt Jones. I was the sixth child of Ruth but the first of Matt, even though he loved Ruth's other children as if they were his, at least that was how it seemed. In time the truth would come out, but for now things were great.

A year later, another child was born. His name was Jerome. Jerome's birth gave Matt a different look on life. Here is another child born out of wedlock, this is not right, Matt thought to himself. I need to do the right thing by Ruth.

See, loving Ruth wasn't the issue, and he knew that she loved him. He didn't want to hurt her, the way those other men did. Sometimes, as he and Ruth talked about her other children, he noticed the pain in her voice when she talked about how they treated her.

He didn't want to be another one of those men. He wanted to marry her, but he didn't have a place for her and her family to stay. In the end, he decided to ask her to marry him anyway. So one warm night as they walked in the park near her home, Matt popped the question, "Ruth, I don't have much to offer you, but I do love you with my whole heart, and I will love your other children as my own."

You know that I'm a very hard worker, and I will do my best to take care of you and the family. So, will you please do me the honor of marrying me?" Ruth was so happy, before she knew it a big yes popped out.

"Yes! I'll marry you!" Ruth replied, with a big smile on her face and tears running down her cheeks, because Matt just asked her the question for which she had been waiting so long. She knew having children outside of marriage was wrong.

Ruth grew up in a church, where the preachers and the mothers taught them that sex outside of marriage was wrong, men always said words that made her feel beautiful. Well, until they got what they wanted. When they learned that she was pregnant they would always leave her with the child. This made her feel betrayed. All she wanted was somebody to love her. Was that so hard?

Matt's proposal made her very happy, and made her felt so beautiful just to know that someone wanted to marry her. At that time and for that moment, all you could hear was the sound of Ruth's heart beating like a drum.

She was so excited that she opened her mouth and asked, "When Matt? When are we getting married?" Matt looked at the excitement on her face, but couldn't give her an answer. The only thing he said was, "Soon, Ruth, very soon." As they walked in the park that night, Matt did not want to let Ruth know that he didn't have any idea where they were going to live.

As days turned to weeks and weeks turned to months, the date for the wedding still wasn't set. One day, as Ruth sat in a chair near the window of her house, she became very ill, an illness that she knew very well. She thought to herself, "No, no not again!" Well, it was true; yes, she was pregnant again.

Ruth sat there with tears rolling down her face. "What is wrong with me?" she thought. "Why am I always doing this to myself? Babies, on top of babies. Now what am I going to do?"

She thought about the engagement between Matt and herself, "Well I guess I need to have a serious talk with Matt to tell him the news," but then she began to think harder about all the men that came and went as soon as they knew she was with child.

"Well, I guess Matt will be the next to leave me after I tell him about this," she thought. "He may think I'm trying to trap him into getting married sooner then he wants to." Just as she was about to leave, there was a knock at her door. It was Matt.

"Hi Matt! I was just thinking about you," she said in a low voice.

"About what?" Matt replied. "And why do you sound so sad?" Matt replied. "Oh nothing, everything is okay" she responded, but Matt sensed that something was wrong. Ruth or Matt didn't say anything for a while; they sat looking at one another, not knowing what to say.

Matt finally opened up and said, "Ruth, I don't know how to put this, but the only thing I can say is that I have a job offer out of town for about a year and a half. I need the money so we can get married, and a man offered me this job with a very good salary and I think I'm going to take it."

Without thinking, Ruth yelled out with a loud voice, "Matt! Matt! You must be kidding me! No! No, you can't go! You just can't!" she cried out as if her world was coming to an end. "What is wrong with you? And why are you crying and yelling like that?" he asked her.

"Matt I didn't want to tell you like this, but I'm pregnant again," she replied. "What! What did you say?" he yelled.

"Yes I am," she said in a sad voice.

"No, Ruth! Not again, you've got to be kidding me!" With those words Matt walked out, slamming the door behind him. As Matt walked away,

Ruth felt as though someone had taken a razor and cut her heart open. Here she is with two small children, carrying another child besides her other children, and her man just walked out on her.

Ruth crying about Matt leaving her

She cried for weeks and weeks, until it seemed as though she had no more tears left. After all that crying she took a long look at herself in the mirror, and she decided that her children needed her and she needed them.

So for her children's sake, she got up to take care of herself and her family. By this time, her mother, Grandma May, told Ruth that she would help her out the best she could. So Ruth decided that the older ones, Stephanie, Bill, and Terry, would stay with their Grandma until she was able to find a place to stay and able to get on her feet.

A few months passed, and Grandma May asked Ruth if she would allow Terry to go live with her Aunt Pearl. Aunt Pearl was grandma May's sister, and she lived alone. This didn't help Ruth feel any better; she wanted her children to stay together. But she knew that Grandma wouldn't be able to take care of all of them after a while. So with a broken heart, she sent Terry to live with her Aunt Pearl.

As the months passed, the day came for Ruth to deliver her baby. As she laid there in her bed, wishing that Matt was there to see what a handsome baby boy they had, she held him so close that her tears wet his tiny little face. "What should I name you?" she asked that tiny baby boy.

"I know! I'll call you Mark, for you have put a mark on my heart today, and you have made all my problems disappear for now." But by the time Mark reached the age of two months, she knew something was wrong. Ruth was always taking him back and forth to the doctor, but the doctor couldn't diagnose his problem.

One warm day in April, after taking her midday nap, Ruth checked on Mark, but something wasn't right: he wasn't moving or breathing. Ruth began screaming, "No, Lord! Not my baby. No, not my baby!

Please Lord don't take him from me!" But Mark was gone. Ruth was so sad; she even began to question God. "Lord how much more do I have to take?" she asked. Am I here just for pain and suffering? Lord, help me please help me!" Ruth cried out with a broken heart.

See, sometimes things happen in our lives that we may not understand at that time, but when God is trying to get our attention and we don't want to listen, we often have to suffer through unnecessary things. All God wanted Ruth to do was to give her life to Him, but Ruth wasn't ready to do that; she wanted to marry Matt first.

In time Ruth felt better, and one day she was sitting in her yard playing with her children she noticed someone coming toward her. At first, she didn't recognize who it was, until I began to yell, "Daddy! Daddy! Mom it's Daddy!" It was Matt. Ruth jumped up with excitement and ran to meet him. They were so happy to see one another that Ruth held him tight for a long time. Then she began to tell him all that had happened while he was out of town. She cried as she talked, and it seemed like her tears weren't going to stop. As Ruth talked, tears rolled down Matt's face as if he was reliving all that had happened.

"Ruth, I'm so sorry, baby, that you went through all of that by yourself." Matt responded. Ruth felt better now that she had someone with whom she could share her pain. A few months later, on a very hot summer day in

July, they were married. After the wedding, Matt told his new wife that he wasn't able to find a place for them to stay, but he would continue to look.

She looked at him, "Well what are we going to do? Where will we stay, Matt?" "Don't worry, I've talked with my mother about us staying with her until I find a place. She said it was okay for now." Matt replied.

For Matt to ask this of his mother was very hard for him to do, but he swallowed his pride and asked anyway. Ruth didn't like the idea of not having a place of their own, but staying with his mother, Grandma Sharon would have to do for now. Besides, Sharon loved Ruth.

But Matt was a different story; his mother would put him down daily, which made him feel very bad and less of a man. "You are no good," Matt's mother said day in and day out, "I don't know why Ruth married you in the first place," she must have felt sorry for you."

Ruth felt the pain of her husband. She tried comforting him daily, and it helped sometimes. The days were not so bad, he just stayed away from the house, but the nights were long and hard on him. He would come in and go straight to the bedroom, trying to avoid his mother. But there she was like a fly humming in his ears. "Oh you just come in and don't say anything." She would say, "This is my house and I'm your mother, talk to me." There was no rest for him.

Dealing with his mother began to get the best of him, and he started drinking, trying to hide all the pain he was feeling. He drank all the time. The liquor bottle became his best friend. His drinking got so bad that his mother finally told us that we had to find another place to stay.

It took a while, but Mom was able to find a tiny four-room house on a hill; it had no indoor plumbing, electricity, phone, or running water, and it looked like a hard wind could blow it over at any time.

But it was our home, and Mom was happy to have one of her own. We didn't have much to start out with, but we made the best of the little we had at that time. For cooking and heating we used a stove that burned wood and coal. Mom and Dad were very happy, especially Mom since she was able to have all except Terry he continual living with Aunt Pearl.

Dad wasn't drinking as much now that we had a place of our own. Sometimes, late in the evening, dad would talk about his childhood, and how bad it was growing up with his sisters, brothers, and mother.

He would always say that his mother took her anger out on her children because their father walked out on them, and she had to struggle to take care of them. She started drinking when they were young, and when she had too much she would take it out on them.

Mom listened as he poured his heart out to her. After each talk, she realized that all she had been though was nothing compared to what Dad had experienced. All she could do was be there for him when he needed to talk.

But then he stopped talking and started drinking again, and things started to change: that childhood abuse from which he suffered began to eat at him, to the point that it started to show. He became so abusive toward Mom and the family that at times it seemed like that love he said he had for his family wasn't there anymore.

That beautiful smile Mom used to wear was gone. Although Dad was a hard worker, it no longer mattered because he drank up all his wages. Drinking became his best friend, family, and food. Things were going down fast, food was short, and Mom didn't want to ask anyone for help.

So she knew what she had to do, and she got a job working extra hard to put food on the table for her family. There were so many days she went without, because it wasn't enough for her and her children.

Still, Mom wasn't thinking about herself, she just wanted to make sure her children had something to eat. Many nights we would find her eating rice crust out of the pot, and her weight eventually went down to ninety-five pounds.

But this didn't bother her, she kept on working very hard. Each morning she got up to go to a job she hated. She was even abused, but wouldn't tell anyone about it, because she needed to work in order to take care of her family and put food on the table.

Grandma May loved her grandchildren, she enjoyed doing and looking out for them. Being at Grandma's house was always an enjoyment but there were times when we sat there on her porch wondering why Mom was taking so long to get home.

There are days I would sat there, looking down that long, lonely road, I noticed a small head coming up over the hill.

It was Mom, a small but graceful woman, trying to make it home; where her next job, cooking, cleaning, and caring for her family was waiting.

The evenings in our home were unpredictable. If our father was drinking, it would be a nightmare for everyone in the house. We were all afraid of that unknown, so we would all sigh with relief to see that Dad wasn't drinking, knowing it would be a good night.

There were nights, not many, when our family would come together to sing while Dad played on his guitar. One thing was for sure, he loved playing that guitar and singing. Just looking at him you knew he was a good man who loved his family, if only he could just stop the drinking.

Matt having a great day playing and singing with his guitar

One thing we found out was Dad was a very smart man; he taught us different word games; and with everything going on, we didn't realize the fact that we were poor. To us there was always something to eat, even if it wasn't what we wanted.

After all we didn't know where the food was coming from, even though now, I can recall a few times our mother left the house to go over to Grandma May's house, and when she returned home there was food for us to eat.

Our family was sheltered by other members of the family that lived around us. We were blessed people living in the midst of many praying, faithful family members. One Saturday evening, Mom was in the kitchen singing like she never sang before.

She seemed so happy, as she sang tears were rolling down the sides of her face. Jerome began crying, and when Mom noticed him she asked, "What is wrong baby…why are you crying?"

"I'm crying because you are," he replied.

"But I'm crying tears of joy, God has been so good to our family, and I'm singing a song of joy. Because of all his blessing." she explained to him. "Oh, I see. Is that why you are going to church all the time now? "asked Jerome.

"Yes! Baby I've given my life to him now he is in control of it. God saved me, now I have joined in with the other family members to help shelter the family, and all those that lives around us in prayer."

Chapter 2

Step in Line

In our neighborhood Sunday morning was a time to remember. Every Sunday at about 5:30 AM, neither rain, snow, or ice could stop this "sunrise" prayer from happening as it traveled from one family house to another. As children, we didn't understand what was going on; all we knew was that we had to be there, for two reasons, that prayer made things better for the family and we had no choice.

This prayer lasted for many years and although Dad never attended any of the prayers, even when they were at our house. After prayer we were allowed to go home for a few hours of sleep before Sunday School.

For some reason, the family had to move to another house, but it wasn't far from the other. The tiny house sat on a hill, with black tar paper all around it with high steps in front and back, and just like the other house, it was home to us.

One-day Dad came home with a surprise: it was a puppy. We were so happy to have a puppy. We named him Tiger, and he became our best friend.

One morning while outside playing with Tiger, our oldest sister Stephanie walked up, looked at the puppy, and asked, "Where did he come from?"

"Dad brought him home today, isn't he beautiful"? Jerome asked "Yes" she replied.

For some reason, Stephanie didn't sleep in the same house as we did, and we didn't understand why our Mom didn't want her to stay with us. During the day she was always at the house with us, but at night she went back to Grandma May's house. Our older brother, Bill, lived with us. He and Stephanie loved taking care of their siblings: they played games, and sometimes cooked for us.

It was fun to have them around especially on the weekends. But then it came time for them to go to school, which made me very sad. I thought that they weren't coming back.

"Jackie, What is wrong with you?" asked Bill, seeing the sad expression on my face.

"I don't want you and Steph to leave me," I replied. "But we'll be back soon." Bill replied.

This didn't make me feel any better. I wanted to follow them.

"You know Jackie; in about a year you'll be old enough to go with us," Steph replied.

"Really!" I responded, "Okay."

Well that day came for me at the age of six. One morning a big yellow bus pulled up to pick us up for school. As I looked at the bus, fear suddenly set in, and I found myself backing up; I couldn't even bear to think about leaving home.

This is a big bus; Jackie is going to school for the first time

I started crying. Bill and Stephanie were very understanding. "Come on Jackie," taking me by the hand, "We're not going to let anything happen to you, okay?" replied Bill.

"Jackie, you're going to have so much fun in school, you'll see," added Steph.

By the end of the day, I was having so much fun I wanted to stay a little longer, but it was time to go. At the sound of the bell, Bill was at the door waiting for me, "Hi, Jackie! Tell me, what did you think about school?" he asked. "Oh, Bill, it was so much fun! I like school!"

"Great. Come on, let's find Steph before we miss our bus." As we walked outside, I heard someone calling Bill's name.

"Bill! Bill! Come on the bus is about to pull out," yelled Steph. "Okay, we're coming, tell the driver not to leave us."

As Bill and I stepped on the bus, Steph was in a hurry to know. "Well... Well!" she said.

"Well... What?" asked Bill.

"How was Jackie's first day at school?" "She had a very good—"

Before Bill finished speaking I stopped him.

"No! Bill! Let me tell her," I said. "Oh, Steph, it was so much fun! We played with clay and played some games. We played outside on the playground, and the teacher even taught us some songs," I exclaimed. "Oh, please! May I go again?"

"Yes, Jackie, today is the beginning of a long time in school. But, in a few years I bet you won't ask to go so often then. Just wait and see," replied Steph.

Playing with Jackie and Jerome

Shortly after my eighth birthday, something strange happened. One day Jerome and I were outside sitting on the back steps playing with Tiger, when we noticed how big our Mom's tummy was getting, not knowing that another brother would soon be here.

Jackie playing with Tiger

Well, one very hot summer night, a cry of pain came from Mom's mouth, a cry we had never heard before. It was so frightening to hear her cry out like that, we didn't know what was going on. "Bill!" I cried out, "Something is wrong with Mom, please go see what's wrong." Just as Bill walked to the front of the house, Dad was walking out of their bedroom.

"Good, Bill you're here. I need to get a ride for your mother to take her to the hospital, and I need you to stay here with the other kids, okay?" Dad asked Bill.

"No problem, I'll be here," Bill replied. Dad left the house to get a ride, and before long he was back with Uncle Pete (Mom's brother). They helped mom out the door and they all left together.

"Bill, take care of them. Take them to your Grandma's house, and I'll be back soon, okay?" Mom said with a very soft voice. As they walked away, Jerome and I began to cry, not knowing what was happening to our mother.

Bill looked at us, noticed how sad we were, and bent over to give us a big hug to comfort us.

The fear that something was happening to our Mom was more than we could bare.

"Don't worry, Mom will be home soon," said Bill, and with those words he took us by the hand, and took us to Grandma May's house.

Chapter 3

No Joke

A few days later, Mom was home with a new baby boy, named Tim. I looked at him and thought to myself, that he was the most beautiful baby I had ever seen. Jerome looked at me and said, "Jackie, something is wrong with his eyes, they look funny."

"Bill! I called out, "Is anything wrong with the baby's eyes? Jerome said they eyes look funny" "All baby eyes look like that," Bill replied. Jerome and I both said at the same time. "They do?"

It didn't matter how his eyes looked, we loved our new baby brother, but at this time Tim didn't have a bed to sleep in. Mom looked at Dad and said, "We need to find something for Tim to sleep in, Matt."

"Yes, I know, but what? We have no money."

"Well, I'll look around the house to see what I can find," Mom said, as she walked through the house looking. Mom said maybe someone may have a box that I can use. So she sent Bill out looking. In about an hour he came home with a nice size cardboard box, thank you Bill this is nice and clean. So she put a pillow in it and made a cradle for the new baby to sleep in.

After Tim turned about one month old, Mom had to go back to work. She wasn't happy about leaving her new baby, but she knew that the only way for us to survive was by her working. She worked for a rich family called the Grants; it seemed like that family loved her, but for some reason she didn't like working for them.

Before leaving in the morning, she would give Bill instructions on taking care of baby Tim, Jerome, and me. Bill knew if something came up that he couldn't handle, all he had to do was call on Grandma May, and she would be there for him. Bill would often send us outside to play, but one day, something happened that I will never forget as long as I live.

As we played with our dog Tiger, Steph decided that she wanted Bill to come outside and play with us as well, but he wouldn't because he was watching Tim inside.

"I know what I'll do, watch this," said Steph "Bill! Bill!" she called, "Come out here! I want to show you something." Just as Bill walked out the door, we jumped him, but Bill was strong, and wrested us all to the ground. "Okay, Bill, we give up," said Steph, and Bill walked back into the house.

Just then, Steph stopped playing and stood in place, looking around as if something was wrong. I looked at her with fear, because the look on her face was frightening. All of a sudden, she cried out, "Bill! I smell something!" "Oh, Steph, what is it now?" Bill replied.

"But, Bill, I smell something!" she yelled. As Steph was speaking, smoke was coming from the side of that old house.

"Our house is on fire!" she yelled.

Smoke coming out of the house/ but the house was save this time

17

Steph, stop playing! I'm trying to take care of Tim. I'll come out but no joking around," he said in a very serious voice, but just as he walked out of the door, he noticed the smoke coming from the side of the house.

"Oh my God, Steph, you're right! Here, watch Jackie and Jerome," he said, and without thinking, Bill ran back into the house picked up that cardboard box that Tim was sleeping in, and ran outside where we were.

"Here, Steph, watch him and let me see what I can do to put out the fire, Bill said, running inside.

"Bill, what can I do to help you?" asked Steph.

"No, Steph you watch them, I have it." Bill was out of sight for a few minutes, but it seemed as though he was gone for hours. Finally, Bill showed up. "It's out," he said, "It was only a small fire. Everything is all right," said Bill.

"Oh, Bill, I'm so happy that the fire didn't burn down our home. Do you know what caused it, Bill?" asked Steph. "It was a small spark from the fire in the stove, I think. The door was left open just a little." Bill answered.

Seeing the way Bill looked after us, we knew that he loved us. He was always doing things for us, even if we didn't understand, but he was our big brother and we loved him too. If Mom needed his help he was there, too. It was like he knew everything that was happening in the house, or maybe it was because he was the oldest and their Mom told him some things.

One of the best days of the year was coming, and it was coming fast: Christmas was on the way. Jerome and I were playing outside with Steph and Bill a few weeks before the big day, and they both asked us what we wanted for Christmas.

"Well, I want a new bicycle!" Jerome yelled.

"Oh, boy, me too!" I said with so much excitement.

"I'll tell you both, then, that if you be good and pray hard, Santa Claus may bring you what you want," Bill said with a big smile on his face.

Mom was working extra hours each day, because she knew we would be looking for some toys under the Christmas tree. Since our house didn't have any electricity, we couldn't have a tree with lights like Uncle Pete and Grandma, who even have a TV and a phone. I often wondered to myself why we couldn't have these things, but we were happy, and I guess that's what counts. Still, I wondered how we were going to pull off a tree without lights.

But to my surprise, there in the corner of the living room was a green pine tree.

"Great, we have a tree, but what about the lights?" I asked Jerome Just before Jerome responded to my question Bill and Steph walked in.

"Come on, we'll show you how to decorate this tree," they both said. "We will need some white paper, flour, and some water," Bill said. But Mom already had everything they needed set aside for them to use.

"Come on, sit here, Jerome, and Jackie, you sit in this chair," Steph said.

As we sat on the chairs, we were looking up to our big, strong brother and our big sister to lead and guide us. It didn't seem to bother them, for they enjoyed seeing the smiles on our faces. Bill and Steph began cutting up paper, and afterward Bill mixed the flour and water together. Jerome and I looked at one another, wondering what in the world they were doing.

"Bill, are you going to make us some pancakes to eat?" asked Jerome. "No, why would you ask me that?"

"Well you're mixing up the flour and the water, and that's what Mom does for pancakes," replied Jerome. "No, we're going to show you how to make glue with the flour and water, okay."

"Okay, how?"

"Just wait, Jerome, I'll show you," Bill said. Bill made a few rings, then he showed us how to do it; we all were working hard and having fun together. "Steph, stop! What are you doing?" Bill suddenly yelled. Steph had put flour all over his face.

"Oh, so you want to play? How about this?" Bill said as he threw flour all over Steph. I looked at them, and they were having so much fun that I decided to join in on the fun too.

I picked up some flour and threw it on Jerome. "Oh no! Jackie! So you want to play like that?"

"Well you asked for it!"

We all threw flour back and forth until Mom walked in.

"What in the world is going on here?" "Stop and clean up this mess now."

But as she walked away she was smiling because she was happy we were having some fun. Not only that, she picked up some flour and threw it on Bill and Steph. We all laughed. The paper rings came out just perfect.

"Our tree looks great with all those white paper rings." said Jerome. "Now that we are done, Bill, what's next?" asked Jerome.

"Well, Jerome, you and Jackie need to go to bed. "Why?" I asked.

"Because, if Santa Claus sees you, he will spit in your eyes and you'll be blind for life" replied Bill.

"Steph, is that true?" asking as I rubbed my sleepy eyes.

"Oh yes! It happened to a boy I know that lives a few streets over, so come on, get in bed."

"Because we don't want that to happen to you. Okay?" Bill replies as he and Steph put us to bed. The night seemed to last forever. The sounds of that night seemed louder than before.

"Jackie are you asleep yet?" Jerome asked.

"No, I'm trying to keep my eyes closed tight." I replied. But sometime during the night, we fell asleep. The sound of the rooster crowing woke us up.

Chapter 4

The Joy

"Jerome! Wake up, it's here! Christmas is here, get up!" I yelled as I jumped out of bed and ran to take my place in front of the Christmas tree. Waiting to see what Santa brought me was almost unbearable, as I called out again, "Come on! Please, come on."

Just then Jerome and Bill walked in. "Where are Mom and Dad?" asked Jerome.

"Here we are," answered Mom, as she walked in the room with a big smile on her face and Tim in her arms. As I looked at our mom's smile; I got a warm feeling inside, because it usually took a lot for her to smile

So at that moment, it seemed as though the whole world was smiling, too. Mom was really one of a kind, and after God made her, he threw away that plan. She always tried to make Christmas a happy time for her family, and even though we didn't have much this Christmas, Mom still surprised us.

As we sat there opening up our toys, Dad walked out and went back to their room. In a short time, he came out, but this time he walked back with a new bike for Jerome and me to share. "We knew that you both wanted a bike for Christmas," Mom said, so here. We love you both, enjoy."

Jerome and I were so happy. "Thank you Mom and Dad, we love it!" we both said. We told our Dad thanks, too, but we knew who bought the bike for us. "Mom, we don't know how to ride a bike, who is going to teach us?" I asked, looking at Bill.

"Come on, I'll show you," replied Bill. I just knew that he would help us.

"Bill, you're not going to let us fall, are you?" I asked while running outside. "Jackie! Jackie! Come back in here and put on a coat and a hat, it's cold out there. You too, Jerome," yelled Mom.

"Okay Mom!" After putting on our hats and coats we ran off. I called out to Bill, "Come on, Bill come on, we are ready!"

"Okay, Jackie, you're first. Hold on."

"Hold me, and don't let me fall, Bill," I said nervously. "Oh girl, get on and hold on: Now peddle, peddle." After about ten minutes of holding, Bill said, "This time don't look at me, just hold on and look straight ahead—Now peddle! Come on, peddle!"

I kept on peddling, thinking that Bill was still holding onto the back of my bike, and kept on riding. Bill yelled with excitement, "Jackie, you're riding, you're doing it all by yourself! Great job!"

"What!" I yelled.

"Look out Jackie!" yelled Jerome, and at that moment I fell, skinned my knees, and cut my hand.

"Are you okay Jackie?" asked Bill.

"You promised that you weren't going to let me fall. And that you were going to hold me! Now look at me!" I replied, as tears were running down my face.

"Don't cry. I'm sorry, but sometime this happens," Bill said.

"But it wasn't supposed to happen to me! No! Not me," I said crying uncontrollably.

"Please, stop crying, Jackie, let me look at your knees, and hands," Bill said. "Okay, see it really hurts," I said, still sniffling.

"I know that it hurts, and I'm so sorry, sis." After looking at my bruises, Bill hugged me for comfort. "Come on let's try again," he said.

"No! I'm going to show Mom!"

"I'll put something on it to help it feel better, Jackie," and then I want you to try again, because you were doing so well. This time I will not let anything bad happen to you, I promise." said Bill.

"No! Bill I don't want to ride anymore today,"

"Well, okay, let Jerome ride," Bill said, turning to our younger brother. "Come on Jerome," said Bill.

Jerome took one look at my scraped hands and knees and said, "Oh no! Not, me!" and then ran into the house.

Bill is teaching Jackie how to ride a bike

Chapter 5

Growing Wings

The next morning, a strange thing happened, something we had never seen before. The ground was covered with white grass, or at least that's what we thought it was.

"Momma! Momma! We have white grass outside," yelled Jerome, "Come here! Mom, it's so beautiful."

The way Jerome was carrying on, I decided to go outside to see what on earth he was talking about. "Boy, what are you yelling so much about?" I asked him.

"Here let me show you. Look see the grass is white! "

"Oh, my! It's true, Momma! Our yard does have white grass," I said with excitement.

"See I told you." Jerome replied.

Mom walked to the door to see what was going on, and with a smile on her face, she said in a very soft voice, "No, babies, that's what we call snow, not white grass."

I looked up at Mom, with a puzzled look on my face, "Snow? Mom, what is snow?"

She explained that snow was made from white crystals of ice that form when water vapor freezes in the air and then falls from the sky to the ground as snow.

But, Mom, what's vapor?" asked Jerome

"Well son, let me see, do you remember how the pot boils when I'm cooking?"

"Yes," he replied.

"Well the mist, or steam, it's like the water in the air, and that gets very, very cold and freezes like ice," Mom explained.

"Okay, I see," he said.

"Mom, God is wonderful to have something so beautiful come down from the sky that looks like white grass," I added.

With a smile on her face she said. "Yes, he is wonderful. Now come on, let me help with your coats, I have to take you to your Grandma's house. My ride will be here soon to pick me up for work." "Oh yes grandma's house, oh yes let's go," replied Jerome.

Grandma was a good lady, and she was the backbone of our family. She lived with her son, Uncle Pete, his wife, Aunt Betty, and their children Uncle Pete, Aunt Betty, and Grandma May were all preachers. They were good people who looked after us while mom was at work.

After mom got off, she would pick us up and take us home, if Bill didn't do it first. One evening after work, Mom was in the kitchen cooking dinner. Steph, Jerome, and I were sitting around talking and laughing with Bill. Everything was going just fine. On this night Dad didn't come home drunk and we were having a good time together.

But all of a sudden, mom cried out, "Bill! You and Steph take the kids outside. Hurry! Hurry! The house is on fire!" I jumped up, picked up Tim, and ran outside.

House on fire this time we lost everything

25

We were all safe, but as Mom stood there looking at our home on fire she began crying, because everything we owned was in that house. All the surrounding families' members tried to help put the fire out. But this time it didn't work. The house was gone, as well as everything we owned. Dad tried to comfort Mom, without showing how much he was hurting, as well. But we could only stand there and watch as our tiny four-room house burned to the ground.

With no place to go, Uncle Pete invited us to stay with them, and even though Mom didn't want to accept, we had no other place to go. Dad didn't want to stay, so he stayed with his brother.

It was a blessing that in a few days, Mom was able to find another house. It wasn't as close to Grandma May, but it was still within walking distance. By this time, I was about ten, and a half years old.

Living in this house was great, because this time Steph moved in with us. It was nice to have my big sister there with me. Plus, we were able to meet other children our age, besides just family members.

The people from whom we rented were preachers as well; they had a farm with cows, chickens, turkeys, and some other animals. It was my first time ever seeing a guinea; it looked like a cross between a chicken and a pigeon all in one. It was fun living next door. This preacher and his wife went by the names of Bishop and Mother Brown. We went to church with them as well.

Going to church with the Browns was much different than going with my family. Bishop Brown drove a truck without a top on the back, and he would put us in the back of that truck and take us to church. It was so much fun if the weather was nice; the air hitting our faces felt good and always smelled so clean.

On rainy nights, they had a big tent they would put over us to keep us warm and dry. It felt like we were camping out on the way home. They were so good to us, and treated us as though we were their children. They put enough joy in our lives to last for a lifetime.

Sometimes, God puts people in our lives for reasons we don't understand, but as we grow older, we realize that those little things they did for us helped make us better people. For that I'm glad we lived next door to the Bishop and Mother.

Sunday through Friday we had fun playing with the farm animals and on their piano, but Saturday was a holy day for them, so on that day, there wasn't any playing at their house for any of the neighborhood children. Their own children had already grown up and moved away. On this day they didn't do any work, or cooking. The only thing they did was go to church all day, for this was their Sabbath day.

It was good that someone was showing us love beside family members, and the Browns taught us many things. It was so amazing to see how Bishop Brown made syrup from sugarcane. They also enjoyed showing us how to milk cows. The learning never stopped.

Bishop and Mother Brown made us feel safe for some reason. It was a great learning period for us, to see that there was another good side to life, because I witnessed some things that really shocked me.

Having fun on the farm, learning about a new life

Chapter 6

Love Song

Living in this new neighborhood, I found out that there are some people who don't like children as much as the Browns, and who are even out to harm them.

It would be wonderful for parents to know who is living around their homes.

In this neighborhood there was a man by the name of Mr. Lee that frightened all the children, boys, and girls. The parents felt comfortable with him being around, because he was their fruits and vegetables man, and would buy from him once a week, but he had a big problem the parents didn't know about. If they knew, they would have never allowed him to come near their children.

Mr. Lee's big problem was that he loved showing his private parts to little girls and boys. Mom or Dad never told us about people like this, but it made me sick to my stomach, because grown-ups are supposed to take care of children and keep them safe, not hurt them. But he wanted to hurt us.

The next time Mr. Lee did this, we told Bill about the naked part of Mr. Lee's body. Bill told us to stay away from him, and if we saw him again to run home as fast as we can, because Mr. Lee was a very bad person. So we did just as we were told.

We played together with the other children, and we had so much fun. Just having other children to play with besides family members was great, and we had such a good time at this point in our lives. Mom and Dad rented from Bishop and Mother Brown for about two and a half years, but by this time, Mom was beginning to miss her family.

Since we moved, the Morning Prayer was cut out and Mom wanted to get us back in prayer.

One-day Mom told us we were going to move again. She found another house closer to Grandma May.

"But Mom, we are going to miss our new friends and Bishop and Mother Brown," said Steph.

"We don't want to move, not now Mom, please not now!" I said in a very sad voice.

Mom replied sincerely, "I understand, Jackie, but I will feel better if you all were closer to my Mom. Not only that, but for other reasons as well."

"What do you mean?" asked Steph.

"Okay, come here and sit down. I need to tell you, your sister, and brothers something, but I'm afraid that you won't understand."

"Tell us what?" asked Steph "Well, Bill will be leaving," Mom began to say. "Leaving! What do you mean he's leaving?"

"Let me finish Steph, okay? He's going off to school for a while." "But Mom, Bill and I go to school together."

"I know that, but he wants to go to another school to take up a new trade, in order to make more money." I looked at Jerome and he looked at me and we both began to cry.

Oh why, did Bill leave me. Why? I want my big brother

"Don't cry, it's not like he won't be back, it's only for one year," said Mom.

"Besides, living by my mother will be the best thing for now."

So, we all packed up, for the move. The new house was better than the last two houses we stayed in. It didn't have indoor plumbing, but it had electricity which was great.

This house looked so much better, too, outside and inside, and being close to the family was nice. Each night before going to bed, we had to make sure water was in the house for the night, so we would walk to the water pump at Grandma May's house.

Mom was even able to cook on a wooden stove, and the food was so good, but things were slowly beginning to change. I was now twelve and a half, and Jerome was eleven and a half years old.

Our big brother Bill, wasn't there to protect us anymore, and we missed him a lot, but our lives were about to be altered in so many ways, good as well as bad and I had no idea how much. But we had to go on without him.

One of the best things about living by Grandma May was watching how she grew things. She had a small farm on side of their house where she grew sweet potatoes, tomatoes, watermelons, greens, green beans, and corn. There were also all kinds of fruits trees to eat from, as well as nut trees.

Summertime was great, with the beautiful cut green grass, and the smell of fresh flowers that filled the air.

The third Sunday of each month was family time. The Saturday before that Sunday, Grandma May, would ask Uncle Pete to kill about four or five chickens for Sunday dinner.

About four weeks before, Grandma would remove the chickens to be killed, and put them in a place all by themselves; this process was called the cleaning-out period. After this period was up, Uncle Pete took the chickens, one by one, from their place, and tied their legs together.

He took each one by the neck and laid it on a chopping block, while another adult held it in place. The sound of the ax hitting each chicken neck rang out. It was always sad to see the chicken hopping around making painful sounds, but on the other side of the yard, Grandma had a big pot with hot water waiting.

Once the chicken stop moving, we were told to put them in the hot water, and when the feathers were soft enough we plucked them off of each chicken one at a time. The smell of wet chicken feathers was sickening, but afterward Aunt Betty finished the cleaning process by putting each chicken over a fire to burn off the extra feathers, they looked like they came from the store.

Grandma loved the family, and loved having them over for dinner, so every third weekend was special to me. A house full with family brought us all so much joy.

Chapter 7

The Fear

One Saturday Grandma was frying some chicken in a big frying pan full of hot grease. Her hand hit the edge of the pan, and it fell off the stove and the grease hit her right leg.

Grandma cried out in so much pain, and when Uncle Pete ran in to see what was going on, there she was on the floor, holding her leg and crying. Her leg looked like someone took a hot iron to it, and the smell of flesh burning is an odor that I will never forget.

We all began to cry, because she was in so much pain. "Someone call an ambulance!" yelled Mom.

"Okay, I'm doing it now!" replied Aunt Betty. Within minutes the ambulance was at the house.

Uncle Pete and Mom jumped in his car to follow her to the emergency room. I watched as they sped off; I've never seen a car move so fast in my life. At the house we were all waiting by the phone to hear what was happening to Grandma.

Finally, the phone rang; it was Uncle Pete who informed us that she had third degree burns on her leg, but with lot of care she would recover in time.

"I need to go now; the doctor wants to talk with us. I'll call you back," Uncle Pete said as he hung up the phone.

About an hour passed, then the phone rang again, and Aunt Betty answered. It was Uncle Pete once more; he informed us that Grandma would have to stay in the hospital for about two weeks.

We missed seeing her around the house, working in her garden, and cooking, but time went by fast, two weeks were up, and she was home. It was so good to see her.

As time passed, she was at it again, doing work for her family and fellow church members. Even with all that happened to her, it didn't stop her from cooking.

If anything she was doing even more for her family. It is hard to keep a good person down and my grandmother was a good person. Seeing her undying devotion toward her family made me appreciate and respect her even more. No wonder Mom always worked so hard, no matter what.

The love in our family was one of a kind, because it wasn't just shown within the family, but outward toward others as well.

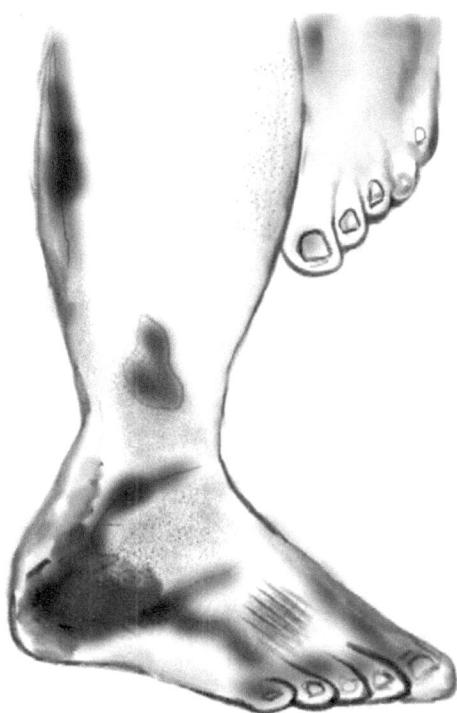

Grandma May is in so much pain, third degree burns

As children, we weren't allowed to talk back to adults, for example. The adults taught us good values, that would help us throughout life.

In spite of knowing this, one day at school my teacher said to me "Jackie, why did you hit Paul on the back of his head"

"But I didn't hit him!" I responded "He said you did."

"I didn't, but you will believe him over me anyway, I said."

"Why are you talking back to me? I am going to send a note home to your mother, by your brother today!" she threatened in an angry voice. She made me so upset, that all of the values that I had learned went right out the window.

Something snapped inside me, and I looked at her and told her she was wrong. I said a few other words as well, and I knew I was wrong for talking back at her, but I was so furious it didn't matter at the time.

Sometimes teachers lie on children, and the children are afraid to speak out, but not me at that time; I knew the truth. As time got closer for school to get out, I was wondering what was going to happen to me. Fear set in as the day went by. but apologizing to my teacher was out of the question.

As I walked down the hall of school, I couldn't help but look around because I felt like the building was going to fall on me. I knew I was in the wrong for talking back to my teacher, even though I was telling her the truth.

As I walked through the front door of our house, I was relieved that Mom didn't say anything to me about me talking back to my teacher in class. I knew she gave my brother a note, but what he did with it I had no idea. I was so happy when Jerome told me that he lost the note, and we didn't have a phone, so I knew the teacher wasn't going to call my Mom.

"Maybe she called Grandma May's," I thought to myself. She did have a phone, that's how Mom received her calls, but it seemed like things were fine. That evening, we were playing outside. About two hours of playing had passed when Mom called us in.

My heart seems to stop for a minute, as I wondered how on earth my teacher were able to get in contact with Mom. Walking in the house, I just knew I was in trouble. All the fun we were having was over now, and I set myself up for what I knew what was about to happen.

"Yes, Mom" answered Steph,

"I need you to go to the store for me," she said, "Take Jackie and Jerome with you." I let out a big sigh of relief. Oh boy she doesn't know anything about what happen in class today, great!

Chapter 8

Love shine through

Mom gave Steph a list of things she wanted, and we started off to the store, playing and talking as we walked down the street. Jerome looked up at Steph and asked, "Steph, how far do we have to walk?"

"It's only about two miles up the street," replied Steph.

"Well if I can't make it, will you pick me up and carry me the rest of the way?"

"Boy, are you crazy? You better walk on your own." I looked at Jerome and we both started to laugh, "I was only playing with you," he said.

We started playing again. "Ouch! That hurt" I yelled. "Jerome, why did you hit me?"

"Hit you? What are you talking about? I didn't hit you"

At that moment I looked down and cried out, "Oh, my God! It's a snake!" "Oh my God!" "Jackie, it's a snake and it bit you on your leg" Yelled Steph. "Jackie, your leg is bleeding!" added Jerome.

"You need to go back home to tell Mom what happened, that a snake bit you. Run! Run! As fast as you can, Jackie!" said Steph, not knowing if she should turn around or continue on to the store.

But she decided that continuing on would be best; so they did. I started off for home, crying. My heart was pounding and I felt awful, but I looked ahead and kept on running.

I ran and didn't stop until I made it home. "Good I made it;" I said to myself. I ran around to the back door. I don't know what was I thinking because the front door was open and Mom and Dad was sitting in the living room talking.

I ran around to the back door. Running in the house, I cried out, "Mom, Dad!" Not only was I in so much pain, I was also very frightened, not knowing what was happening inside my body because of that snake bite. "What! What is wrong," asked Mom.

"A snake bit me on my leg, see," showing her the spot.

"What did you say? A snake!" asked Dad. "Yes Dad, a snake!"

Without thinking, Dad jumped up and went in their room. I looked at him, wondering what he was going to do.

He rushed back in the living room with a razor in his hand. Taking my leg, he cut a cross over the bite and began to suck the bad blood out. I couldn't believe my eyes. Here was my Dad, with all those bad teeth in his mouth was not thinking about his life at all. The only thing that was on his mind was saving his child. I was so scared, I thought I was going to die.

After he was done, he went to ask Uncle Pete to take me to the emergency room. Just like any other time, Uncle Pete came to our aid with no problem.

As Uncle Pete drove up to the hospital, it looked so big from the outside, and I walked inside. It was just as big and all the walls were white. There were so many people, that it scared me. I had never seen so many people in my life before.

But the nurses and doctors were very nice as they talked and worked on me. "Well, Ms. Jacqueline, can you tell me what was the color of the snake?" asked one doctor.

My lips quivered with fear as I spoke to the doctor, "Yes, I think it was orange and black."

"Okay, don't be nervous, I'm not going to hurt you, sweetheart."

For some reason, his words made me feel better. He turned around, and walked out of my room.

"Mommy, I feel funny in my stomach." At that moment I threw up all over the place. Tears rolled down my face.

"Jackie, it's all right," Mom replied, as she washed my face and cleaned me up.

"My stomach feels better now." At that time, the doctor walked back in. Mom told him all about me getting sick.

He looked at me and explained, "Yes, that sickness sometimes happens after a snake bite," but the good news is that the snake wasn't poisonous, and that Jacqueline can go home. The bad news is that for about six weeks she will feel very sick, but in time she will feel better.

"Thank God, and thank you, doctor for what you have done. I'm so thankful it wasn't poisonous," Mom said.

Ouch! That hurts

Chapter 9

Heart and Soul

About two weeks passed, and Bill came home from the job training camp. We were so happy to see him. It seemed as though he was gone for five years, but it was only one. Although I was still sick, I was happy to see him.

He wasn't happy to see his baby sister sick, all the same, he wanted some information about what happen. Mom was in the next room, "Mom!" Bill called out, "What is wrong with Jackie?"

Mom told him all about the snake and how they thought that they were going to lose me. "But we are so thankful to our Lord that she is still with us."

"Oh yes, me too," Bill said as he walked away.

Weeks went by and I was still sick, not being able to eat, and walking hunched over like a very old person. As I sat in my room on the edge of the bed, Bill walked in with a sad face. "How are you?" he asked in a very low voice.

"I'm not feeling very well, Bill."

"I know what will put a smile on your face. I'll be back soon, okay?" said Bill. He left the house quickly and was back in about an hour

"Jackie! I have something for you," Bill called out.

"Okay, Bill, what is it?" Bill walked in the room with his hands behind his back, "Surprise! Here's your favorite cake, angel food!"

"Oh, thank you, Bill! "I'll eat it later."

But a week went by and I still couldn't touch it; I wasn't able to eat anything. As I sat around the house, Bill, Steph, and Jerome started to worry about me. At one point Jerome ran to Mom, crying, "Mom! Is Jackie going to die?" "Oh, no, baby, she will be all right soon, we just have to give her some time and keep praying for her," Mom replied.

"Okay," said Jerome, "I'll keep praying for her."

Bill was the best brother in this world to me. He knew if I didn't eat the cake something was really wrong.

After three weeks, my body started to straighten up. It felt good to stand upright again. I thought that I wasn't going to last one week, but it had been six weeks and I was doing well, glory be to God.

After three months I was my old fun self again, but I learned a big lesson: God sees everything. From that day, I make an effort in watching what I say, not only to adults, but to anyone.

I was feeling great now, and the fun was starting up again. One summer morning, Steph and I were in the kitchen talking while I was washing the dishes, then there was that favorite call. "Steph, will you please cook my favorite dish for me after Jackie is done with the dishes?" asked Bill.

"For you Bill, anything." Bill's favorite dish was pancakes, syrup, and hot chocolate. Left up to him, he would eat and drink this twenty-four seven, but sometimes we just loved playing tricks on him.

In a house without any plumbing, we had to hand wash the dishes in what they called a dishpan. Sometimes the dishwater was left on top of the stove and sitting there it almost looked like hot chocolate.

Well, that day our big brother couldn't wait for Steph to fix his cocoa. "Steph, whose hot cocoa is on the stove, is it mine?"

"What hot cocoa?" Steph replied.

"Never mind, did you cook the pancakes for me?" "Yes, they're on top of the stove." As Bill sat down to eat, Steph noticed that Bill had a big cup of dark liquid. She didn't say a word, only watched him as he enjoyed his meal. "Oh Steph, this tastes so good, thank you!" With those words, he lifted the cup to drink. Tim called out, "Bill! Don't drink that, it's not hot cocoa it's dish water!"

Steph, Jerome, and I felt out laughing; we just laughed and laughed until tears rolled down our faces. At that point all Bill could do was laugh along with us. "Oh, were you going to let me drink that dish water, Steph?"

"No, I would have stopped you before you drank it," replied Step. There were so many fun times growing up, because we loved one another and loved spending time together.

Family time at the dinner table was also surprising because you never knew what Bill had on his mind. Once he's at the table, look out, because he will say and do anything just to get your food. Sunday's evening after church those dinners were the best.

Mom did all she could do to make our dinners special. She could cook the best meal you ever tasted on that wooden stove. Her gingerbread cakes were something you could never forget. Sometimes she would do really special things for us. The way she made things with such tender care, we knew it was love.

One day Mom put this deep pan on the stove, with a lot of cooking oil in it, we thought it was for her famous fried chicken. But to our surprise she made some homemade donuts for us, umm...good.

Mom taught me how to make the most out of whatever I had. She was a woman of very few words, but when she did speak, those words struck a cord in my heart. She taught me that she would always be there to guide me, and that through it all, the love of family is unconditional and unbreakable.

Don't drink that Bill, it's dish water

The end of book 1

www.ingramcontent.com/pod-product-compliance
Lightning Source LLC
Chambersburg PA
CBHW030527130626
46549CB00007B/3130